EASY CUCUMBER COOKBOOK

50 DELICIOUS CUCUMBER RECIPES; METHODS AND TECHNIQUES FOR COOKING WITH CUCUMBERS

By
BookSumo Press
Copyright © by Saxonberg Associates
All rights reserved

Published by
BookSumo Press, a DBA of Saxonberg Associates
http://www.booksumo.com/

ABOUT THE AUTHOR.

BookSumo Press is a publisher of unique, easy, and healthy cookbooks.

Our cookbooks span all topics and all subjects. If you want a deep dive into the possibilities of cooking with any type of ingredient. Then BookSumo Press is your go to place for robust yet simple and delicious cookbooks and recipes. Whether you are looking for great tasting pressure cooker recipes or authentic ethic and cultural food. BookSumo Press has a delicious and easy cookbook for you.

With simple ingredients, and even simpler step-by-step instructions BookSumo cookbooks get everyone in the kitchen chefing delicious meals.

BookSumo is an independent publisher of books operating in the beautiful Garden State (NJ) and our team of chefs and kitchen experts are here to teach, eat, and be merry!

INTRODUCTION

Welcome to *The Effortless Chef Series*! Thank you for taking the time to purchase this cookbook.

Come take a journey into the delights of easy cooking. The point of this cookbook and all BookSumo Press cookbooks is to exemplify the effortless nature of cooking simply.

In this book we focus on Cucumber. You will find that even though the recipes are simple, the taste of the dishes are quite amazing.

So will you take an adventure in simple cooking? If the answer is yes please consult the table of contents to find the dishes you are most interested in.

Once you are ready, jump right in and start cooking.

— BookSumo Press

TABLE OF CONTENTS

About the Author..2

Introduction 3

Table of Contents 4

Any Issues? Contact Us 8

Legal Notes..9

Common Abbreviations 10

Chapter 1: Easy Cucumber Recipes 11

Alfalfa Cucumber Lunch 11

Aunty's Cucumber Slaw 14

North Carolina Slaw 16

Skinny Girl Lunch Box Cucumbers 18

Cucumber Juice 20

Cucumber Festivals 22

Cucumber Spritzer......................................24

Skillet Cucumbers 26

Cucumber Party Topping for Chips 28

Easy Cucumber Cookbook   4

Cucumber Namasu (Japanese Pickled Vegetable Appetizer) 30

Fluffy Cucumbers 32

Cucumber Fizzy Drink 34

Katherine's August Ketchup 36

How to Fry Cucumbers 39

Barcelona Salsa 41

Mediterranean Yogurt Cucumber 43

Alternative Hummus 45

Pre-Colonial Cucumbers 47

Fathia's Falafel 49

Tuesday Night Snack 52

Bangkok Spicy Salad 54

Artisanal Veggie Bread 56

Cajun Cucumbers 59

Montana Ranch Cucumbers 61

White Sauce of Cucumbers 63

Canning Cucumbers 65

Pumpernickel Party Appetizer 67

Stir Fried Kale 69

Cucumber with Seoul (Korean Kimchee)..................72

New England Tilapia with Tarragon 75

Michelle's Cucumber Velvet.................................78

Cucumber Freezies 80

Asian-Fusion Cucumbers....................................82

Country Cabin Cucumbers Side Dish.......................84

Andy's Korean Style Cucumbers with Hot Sauce 87

Japanese Inspired Sesame Cucumbers 89

Cucumber Turkey Bites 91

Winter Harvest Soup 93

Summer Salad of Mint 96

Cucumber Fiesta 98

California Lunch Box Cucumber Treats.................102

Canning Cucumbers in Hong Kong 104

Simply Sushi 106

Asian Cucumber With Noodle 108

3-Brother's Antipasto 111

Cucumber Cayenne Mayo 113

Cream Cheese Cucumber Sauce.........................115

Lunch Box Ranch Sandwiches 117

THANKS FOR READING! JOIN THE CLUB AND KEEP ON COOKING WITH 6 MORE COOKBOOKS.... 119

Come On... 121

Let's Be Friends :).. 121

ANY ISSUES? CONTACT US

If you find that something important to you is missing from this book please contact us at
info@booksumo.com.

We will take your concerns into consideration when the 2nd edition of this book is published. And we will keep you updated!

— BookSumo Press

LEGAL NOTES

ALL RIGHTS RESERVED. NO PART OF THIS BOOK MAY BE REPRODUCED OR TRANSMITTED IN ANY FORM OR BY ANY MEANS. PHOTOCOPYING, POSTING ONLINE, AND / OR DIGITAL COPYING IS STRICTLY PROHIBITED UNLESS WRITTEN PERMISSION IS GRANTED BY THE BOOK'S PUBLISHING COMPANY. LIMITED USE OF THE BOOK'S TEXT IS PERMITTED FOR USE IN REVIEWS WRITTEN FOR THE PUBLIC.

COMMON ABBREVIATIONS

cup(s)	C.
tablespoon	tbsp
teaspoon	tsp
ounce	oz.
pound	lb

*All units used are standard American measurements

CHAPTER 1: EASY CUCUMBER RECIPES

ALFALFA CUCUMBER LUNCH

Ingredients
- 2 thick slices whole wheat bread
- 2 tbsps cream cheese, softened
- 6 slices cucumber
- 2 tbsps alfalfa sprouts
- 1 tsp olive oil
- 1 tsp red wine vinegar
- 1 tomato, sliced
- 1 leaf lettuce
- 1 oz. pepperoncini, sliced
- 1/2 avocado, mashed

Directions
- Lay out two pieces of bread and coat each side evenly with 1 tbsp of cream cheese.
- Place your cucumber pieces evenly on one side of the bread then layer on top of your bread the cucumber then the sprouts then some vinegar and oil. Now top everything with your pepperoncini, lettuce, and tomato slices.
- Coat the other slice of bread with your avocado evenly then place each piece of bread together carefully.

- Enjoy.

Amount per serving 1
Timing Information:

Preparation	10 m
Total Time	10 m

Nutritional Information:

Calories	496 kcal
Fat	32.5 g
Carbohydrates	46.3g
Protein	11.4 g
Cholesterol	32 mg
Sodium	1024 mg

* Percent Daily Values are based on a 2,000 calorie diet.

Aunty' s Cucumber Slaw

Ingredients
- 3 large cucumbers, skin removed, sliced thinly
- 1 tsp salt
- 1/4 C. white sugar
- 1/8 C. water
- 1/4 C. distilled white vinegar
- 1/2 tsp celery seed
- 1/4 C. chopped onion

Directions
- Place you cumber into a casserole dish or bowl and top them with some salt evenly. Leave the cucumber to sit for 40 mins then squeeze the slices to remove any excess liquids.
- Get a 2nd bowl combine: onion, sugar, celery seed, vinegar, and water. Stir the mix then combine in your cucumbers. Stir the mix again evenly then place a covering of plastic on the bowl and put everything in the fridge for 90 mins.
- Enjoy.

Amount per serving 5
Timing Information:

Preparation	40m
Cooking	1h30m
Total Time	2h10m

Nutritional Information:

Calories	68 kcal
Fat	0.2 g
Carbohydrates	17g
Protein	1.2 g
Cholesterol	0 mg
Sodium	469 mg

* Percent Daily Values are based on a 2,000 calorie diet.

NORTH CAROLINA SLAW

Ingredients
- 2 cucumbers - quartered, seeded, and thinly sliced
- 2 carrots, shredded
- 1/4 onion, grated
- 2 tbsps white sugar
- 1 1/2 tsps ground coriander
- 1 tsp kosher salt
- 1/2 tsp coarse ground black pepper
- 1/4 C. apple cider vinegar

Directions
- Get a bowl, evenly mix: black pepper, cucumbers, salt, carrots, coriander, sugar, and onion. Stir the mix completely then combine in the vinegar and stir everything again.
- Enjoy.

Amount per serving 6
Timing Information:

| Preparation | 10 m |
| Total Time | 10 m |

Nutritional Information:

Calories	47 kcal
Fat	0.3 g
Carbohydrates	10.9g
Protein	1 g
Cholesterol	0 mg
Sodium	337 mg

* Percent Daily Values are based on a 2,000 calorie diet.

SKINNY GIRL LUNCH BOX CUCUMBERS

Ingredients
- 1 C. mayonnaise
- 1/4 C. vinegar
- 1/4 C. white sugar
- 1/4 tsp salt
- 4 C. sliced cucumbers

Directions
- Get a bowl, combine: salt, mayo, sugar, and vinegar. Stir the mix completely then combine in the cucumbers and stir the mix again. Place a covering of plastic on the bowl and put everything in the fridge for 2.5 hrs.
- Enjoy.

Amount per serving (8
Timing Information:

Preparation	10 m
Cooking	2h
Total Time	2 h 10 m

Nutritional Information:

Calories	229 kcal
Fat	21.9 g
Carbohydrates	8.6g
Protein	0.6 g
Cholesterol	10 mg
Sodium	230 mg

* Percent Daily Values are based on a 2,000 calorie diet.

CUCUMBER JUICE

Ingredients
- 3 quarts water
- 3 quarts ice cubes
- 1 (.14 oz.) package sugar free instant lemonade powder
- 1 (12 fluid oz.) can white grape juice concentrate
- 1 lemon, sliced
- 1/2 medium cucumber, thinly sliced

Directions
- Get a large bowl, combine evenly: grape juice concentrate, water, lemonade mix, and ice. Stir the juice completely then place your pieces of lemon and cucumber into the juice and let slices float to the top.
- Enjoy.

Amount per serving 12
Timing Information:

Preparation	2 m
Total Time	2 m

Nutritional Information:

Calories	63 kcal
Fat	0.1 g
Carbohydrates	15.8g
Protein	0.3 g
Cholesterol	0 mg
Sodium	17 mg

* Percent Daily Values are based on a 2,000 calorie diet.

CUCUMBER FESTIVALS

Ingredients
- 1 (1 pound) loaf cocktail rye bread
- 1/2 C. mayonnaise
- 2 cucumbers, thinly sliced
- 1 tsp lemon pepper

Directions
- Coat each piece of bread with mayo evenly. Then layer each piece with about 4 pieces of cucumbers. Top each piece with a good amount of lemon pepper then serve.
- Enjoy.

Amount per serving 45
Timing Information:

| Preparation | 20 m |
| Total Time | 20 m |

Nutritional Information:

Calories	19 kcal
Fat	2 g
Carbohydrates	0.4g
Protein	0.1 g
Cholesterol	< 1 mg
Sodium	24 mg

* Percent Daily Values are based on a 2,000 calorie diet.

Cucumber Spritzer

Ingredients
- 2 cucumbers - peeled, seeded, and chopped
- 3/8 C. fresh lime juice
- 1/3 C. white sugar
- 2/3 C. water

Directions
- Add the following to a blender: water, cucumber, sugar, and lime juice.
- Process the mix until it has the thickness of a cooler or puree then pour everything into a pitcher or container.
- Place everything in the fridge until it chilled.
- Enjoy.

Amount per serving 1
Timing Information:

Preparation	10 m
Total Time	10 m

Nutritional Information:

Calories	365 kcal
Fat	0.7 g
Carbohydrates	94.8g
Protein	4 g
Cholesterol	0 mg
Sodium	18 mg

* Percent Daily Values are based on a 2,000 calorie diet.

Skillet Cucumbers

Ingredients
- 1/2 C. butter
- 3 cucumbers - halved lengthwise, seeded, and cut into 1/2-inch slices
- 1 tbsp tarragon
- 1/2 tsp ground white pepper
- salt to taste

Directions
- Get a frying hot with some butter. Once the butter is melted and hot combine in your salt, cucumbers, white pepper, and tarragon.
- Stir fry your cucumbers for about 13 mins. Then place everything onto plates for serving.
- Enjoy.

Amount per serving 4
Timing Information:

Preparation	10 m
Cooking	15 m
Total Time	25 m

Nutritional Information:

Calories	240 kcal
Fat	23.3 g
Carbohydrates	8.5g
Protein	1.9 g
Cholesterol	61 mg
Sodium	265 mg

* Percent Daily Values are based on a 2,000 calorie diet.

Cucumber Party Topping for Chips

Ingredients
- 1 C. sour cream
- 1 C. mayonnaise
- 1 tbsp dried minced onion
- 2 tbsps dried parsley
- 2 tsps dried dill weed
- 2 tsps Beau Monde (TM) seasoning
- 1/4 tsp seasoning salt
- 1/8 tsp ground black pepper

Directions
- Get a bowl, combine evenly: pepper, sour cream, seasoning salt, mayo, Beau Monde, onion, dill weed, and parsley. Stir the mix completely then place a covering of plastic on the bowl and put everything in the fridge throughout the night or for 7 hrs.
- Enjoy.

Amount per serving 20
Timing Information:

Preparation	10m
Cooking	8h
Total Time	8 h 10 m

Nutritional Information:

Calories	105 kcal
Fat	11.2 g
Carbohydrates	1.1g
Protein	0.5 g
Cholesterol	9 mg
Sodium	81 mg

* Percent Daily Values are based on a 2,000 calorie diet.

CUCUMBER NAMASU (JAPANESE PICKLED VEGETABLE APPETIZER)

Ingredients
- 2 large cucumbers, peeled
- 1/3 C. rice vinegar
- 4 tsps white sugar
- 1 tsp salt
- 1 1/2 tsps minced fresh ginger root

Directions
- Lay out each cucumber and cut each one into two pieces lengthwise. With a spoon evenly take out all the seeds from each half. Now with a sharp knife evenly slice each half of cucumber into thin pieces.
- Once all your cucumber has been sliced evenly get a bowl and mix: ginger, vinegar, salt, and sugar. Stir the vinegar mix evenly until everything has dissolved then add in your cucumber and make sure all the pieces are evenly covered with the mix.
- Place a covering of plastic on the bowl and put everything in the fridge for 60 mins.
- Enjoy.

Amount per serving 5
Timing Information:

Preparation	15m
Cooking	1h
Total Time	1 h 15 m

Nutritional Information:

Calories	27 kcal
Fat	0.2 g
Carbohydrates	6.2g
Protein	0.6 g
Cholesterol	0 mg
Sodium	467 mg

* Percent Daily Values are based on a 2,000 calorie diet.

FLUFFY CUCUMBERS

Ingredients
- salt to taste
- 3 cucumbers, peeled and thinly sliced
- 1 (12 oz.) can evaporated milk
- 2 tbsps white vinegar
- ground black pepper, to taste

Directions
- Get a bowl, mix your salt and cucumbers. Let the mix sit for 5 hrs, then remove the excess liquids. With a cloth pick up all the cucumber and squeeze to remove more of the excess liquids.
- Get a 2nd bowl, combine: vinegar and evaporated milk. Stir the mix until it is thick then combine in your cucumber and stir the mix again. Add in some black pepper and stir everything again.
- Enjoy.

Amount per serving 8
Timing Information:

Preparation	20 m
Cooking	3h
Total Time	3 h 20 m

Nutritional Information:

Calories	66 kcal
Fat	3.3 g
Carbohydrates	6.2g
Protein	3.3 g
Cholesterol	12 mg
Sodium	95 mg

* Percent Daily Values are based on a 2,000 calorie diet.

CUCUMBER FIZZY DRINK

Ingredients
- 1 cucumber, thinly sliced
- 1 (12 oz.) can frozen lemonade concentrate
- 1 (2 litre) bottle lemon-lime flavoured carbonated beverage

Directions
- Get a large beverage container and put your cucumber in it. Add in the concentrate and leave everything to sit for 15 mins. Now combine in the soda and stir everything until the concentrate it dissolved evenly.
- Divide the mix between serving glasses.
- Enjoy.

Amount per serving 8
Timing Information:

Preparation	20 m
Total Time	20 m

Nutritional Information:

Calories	207 kcal
Fat	0.1 g
Carbohydrates	53.6g
Protein	0.3 g
Cholesterol	0 mg
Sodium	31 mg

* Percent Daily Values are based on a 2,000 calorie diet.

KATHERINE'S AUGUST KETCHUP

Ingredients
- 3 very large cucumbers - peeled, seeded, and chopped
- 2 large onions, chopped
- 1/2 C. salt
- 1 C. apple cider vinegar
- 1/4 C. mustard seed
- 1 tsp ground black pepper

Directions
- Get a bowl, combine: onions and cucumber. Stir the mix then stir in your salt and get everything evenly combined. Once all the pieces have been coated with salt place everything into a colander and cover the colander with some plastic.
- Leave the mix to sit throughout the night.
- Get a 2nd bowl and pour the cucumber mix into the bowl, then add in your cider vinegar and stir everything evenly.
- With a batch process begin to put some of the cucumber mix into a food processor and puree the mix completely. Once everything has been pureed place it all back into the bowl and combine in your black pepper and mustard seed.

- Stir the pepper and seed into the mix then divide the ketchup between jars. Tightly seal the jars and put everything in the fridge to chill for 4 days.
- Enjoy.

Amount per serving 48
Timing Information:

Preparation	25 m
Cooking	8h
Total Time	8 h 25 m

Nutritional Information:

Calories	10 kcal
Fat	0.3 g
Carbohydrates	1.3g
Protein	0.4 g
Cholesterol	0 mg
Sodium	1164 mg

* Percent Daily Values are based on a 2,000 calorie diet.

HOW TO FRY CUCUMBERS

Ingredients
- 1/2 C. vegetable oil
- 2 cucumbers, peeled and sliced
- 1 C. cornmeal
- salt to taste

Directions
- Get a big frying pan and get your veggie oil hot for frying. Once the oil is hot place some paper towel on a plate and get a dish for your cornmeal.
- Coat your pieces of cucumber with the cornmeal evenly then begin to fry the pieces for about 2 to 3 mins each side. Once the cumbers have been fried completely and are golden place then on the paper towel lined plate and top everything with salt evenly.
- Enjoy.

Amount per serving 4
Timing Information:

Preparation	15 m
Cooking	10 m
Total Time	25 m

Nutritional Information:

Calories	391 kcal
Fat	28.3 g
Carbohydrates	32.4g
Protein	3.4 g
Cholesterol	0 mg
Sodium	102 mg

* Percent Daily Values are based on a 2,000 calorie diet.

Barcelona Salsa

Ingredients
- 2 cucumbers - peeled, seeded and chopped
- 1 C. sour cream
- 1 C. plain yogurt
- 1/4 C. chopped fresh parsley
- 1/4 C. chopped fresh cilantro
- 1 tsp ground cumin
- 1/2 tsp salt

Directions
- Get a bowl, combine: salt, cucumber, cumin, sour cream, cilantro, parsley and yogurt. Stir the mix completely to form a salsa then place a covering of plastic on the bowl and put everything in the fridge for 4 hours.
- Enjoy.

Amount per serving 48
Timing Information:

Preparation	15m
Cooking	2h
Total Time	2h15m

Nutritional Information:

Calories	15 kcal
Fat	1.1 g
Carbohydrates	0.8g
Protein	0.5 g
Cholesterol	2 mg
Sodium	31 mg

* Percent Daily Values are based on a 2,000 calorie diet.

MEDITERRANEAN YOGURT CUCUMBER

Ingredients
- 2 hot house cucumber - peeled, seeded and thinly sliced
- 2 C. Greek yogurt
- 3 tbsps lemon juice
- 2 tbsps chopped fresh mint
- 1/2 tsp white sugar
- 1/4 tsp kosher salt
-

Directions
- Get a bowl, combine: salt, cucumber, sugar, yogurt, mint, and lemon juice. Stir the mix completely then place a covering of plastic on the bowl and put everything in the fridge for 7 hours.
- Enjoy.

Amount per serving 12
Timing Information:

Preparation	15m
Cooking	3h
Total Time	3h15m

Nutritional Information:

Calories	50 kcal
Fat	3.3 g
Carbohydrates	2.8g
Protein	2.5 g
Cholesterol	8 mg
Sodium	62 mg

* Percent Daily Values are based on a 2,000 calorie diet.

ALTERNATIVE HUMMUS

Ingredients
- 4 cloves garlic
- 1/4 C. tahini paste, or to taste
- 1 lemon, juiced
- 1 tsp extra-virgin olive oil
- 1 (15 oz.) can garbanzo beans, drained
- 1 cucumber, coarsely chopped
- salt and black pepper to taste
- 1 pinch paprika

Directions
- Add the following to your blender: olive oil, garlic, lemon juice, and tahini. Process everything until your garlic is minced completely then combine in the cucumber and garbanzos. Continue to puree the mix until it resembles a hummus then combine in some pepper and salt to your taste.
- Place everything into a container for storage and place a cover on the container.
- Put everything in the fridge for 3 hours then top the hummus with some paprika.
- Enjoy.

Amount per serving 12
Timing Information:

Preparation	
Cooking	1h
Total Time	1h10m

Nutritional Information:

Calories	68 kcal
Fat	3.4 g
Carbohydrates	8.6g
Protein	2.3 g
Cholesterol	0 mg
Sodium	76 mg

* Percent Daily Values are based on a 2,000 calorie diet.

PRE-COLONIAL CUCUMBERS

Ingredients
- 2 cucumbers, sliced
- 1/4 C. white wine vinegar
- 2 tbsps white sugar
- 2 tsps celery seed
- 1/8 tsp ground black pepper
- 3/4 tsp salt
- 2 tbsps chopped onion
- 1 tbsp lemon juice

Directions
- Get a bowl, combine: lemon juice, cucumber, onion, vinegar, salt, sugar, pepper, and celery seed. Stir the mix completely then place a covering of plastic on the bowl and put the mix in the fridge for 5 hours.
- Enjoy.

Amount per serving 7
Timing Information:

Preparation	10m
Cooking	4h
Total Time	4 h 10 m

Nutritional Information:

Calories	27 kcal
Fat	0.2 g
Carbohydrates	6.4g
Protein	0.5 g
Cholesterol	0 mg
Sodium	252 mg

* Percent Daily Values are based on a 2,000 calorie diet.

FATHIA'S FALAFEL

Ingredients
For Sauce:
- 1 (6 oz.) container plain yogurt
- 1/2 cucumber - peeled, seeded, and finely chopped
- 1 tsp dried dill weed
- salt and pepper to taste
- 1 tbsp mayonnaise (optional)

For Falafel:
- 1 (15 oz.) can chickpeas (garbanzo beans), drained
- 1 onion, chopped
- 1/2 C. fresh parsley
- 2 cloves garlic, chopped
- 1 egg
- 2 tsps ground cumin
- 1 tsp ground coriander
- 1 tsp salt
- 1 dash pepper
- 1 pinch cayenne pepper
- 1 tsp lemon juice
- 1 tsp baking powder
- 1 tbsp olive oil
- 1 C. dry bread crumbs
- oil for frying

- 2 pita breads, cut in half (optional)
- 1 C. chopped tomatoes (optional)

Directions
- Get a bowl, mix evenly: mayo, yogurt, pepper, cucumber, salt, and dill. Place the mix in the fridge for 1 hour.
- Get a 2nd bowl for your chickpeas and begin to work them with a masher until they are paste like.
- Add your garlic, parsley, and onion to a food processor and puree them. Combine the puree with the chickpeas and stir everything together.
- Get a 3rd bowl, combine: baking powder, egg, lemon juice, cumin, cayenne, coriander, pepper, and salt. Combine this mix with the chickpea mix then add in your olive oil as well and stir everything completely.
- Now carefully work in come bread crumbs to the mix so that the mixture can be formed into 8 balls. Only add enough bread crumbs so that the mix will hold together firmly.
- Form eight balls from the mixture then flatten each ball.
- Now get some oil hot in a frying pan with a medium level of heat. Once the oil is hot about 1.5 inches of oil. Begin to cook your patties in the oil until they are golden on each side.
- Place 2 patties on a pita with some diced tomatoes and the yogurt mayo cucumber sauce.
- Enjoy.

Amount per serving 4
Timing Information:

Preparation	20 m
Cooking	10 m
Total Time	1 h

Nutritional Information:

Calories	586 kcal
Fat	33.1 g
Carbohydrates	59.5g
Protein	14.7 g
Cholesterol	50 mg
Sodium	1580 mg

* Percent Daily Values are based on a 2,000 calorie diet.

TUESDAY NIGHT SNACK

Ingredients
- 1 (8 oz.) package cream cheese, softened
- 1 (.7 oz.) package dry Italian-style salad dressing mix
- 1/2 C. mayonnaise
- 1 French baguette, cut into 1/2 inch thick circles
- 1 cucumber, sliced
- 2 tsps dried dill weed

Directions
- Get bowl, combine: mayo, cream cheese, and dressing mix.
- Take one piece of bread and coat it evenly with some of the cheese mix. Place a topping of cucumber on the bread then top everything with some dill.
- Continue preparing each piece of bread in this manner until all the ingredients have been used up.
- Enjoy.

Amount per serving 12
Timing Information:

| Preparation | 15 m |
| Total Time | 15 m |

Nutritional Information:

Calories	247 kcal
Fat	14.5 g
Carbohydrates	23.7g
Protein	6.1 g
Cholesterol	24 mg
Sodium	619 mg

* Percent Daily Values are based on a 2,000 calorie diet.

BANGKOK SPICY SALAD

Ingredients
- 3 large cucumbers, peeled, halved lengthwise, seeded, and cut into 1/4-inch slices
- 1 tbsp salt
- 1/2 C. white sugar
- 1/2 C. rice wine vinegar
- 2 jalapeno peppers, seeded and chopped
- 1/4 C. chopped cilantro
- 1/2 C. chopped peanuts

Directions
- Get a colander and combine in it: salt and cucumber. Let the mix sit for 40 mins. Run the cucumber until cold water then remove the excess liquids.
- Get a bowl, combine evenly: vinegar and sugar. Stir the mix until the sugar is combined completely then combine in the cucumber, cilantro, and jalapenos. Stir the mix evenly then top everything with the peanuts.
- Enjoy.

Amount per serving 4
Timing Information:

Preparation	15m
Cooking	30m
Total Time	45m

Nutritional Information:

Calories	238 kcal
Fat	9.4 g
Carbohydrates	37.1g
Protein	5.8 g
Cholesterol	0 mg
Sodium	1751 mg

* Percent Daily Values are based on a 2,000 calorie diet.

Artisanal Veggie Bread

Ingredients
- cooking spray
- 2 C. peeled, seeded, and shredded cucumber
- 3 eggs
- 1 C. vegetable oil
- 2 C. white sugar
- 1 tsp vanilla extract
- 1 C. coarsely chopped pecans
- 3 C. all-purpose flour
- 1 tbsp ground cinnamon
- 1 tsp baking soda
- 1/2 tsp salt
- 1/4 tsp baking powder
- 1/8 tsp ground nutmeg
- 1/8 tsp ground cloves

Directions
- Coat 2 bread pan with non-stick spray then set your oven to 325 degrees before doing anything else.
- Get a colander and let your shredded cucumber sit in it for 40 mins.
- Get a bowl, combine: pecans, eggs, cucumber, veggie oil, vanilla, and sugar.

- Get a 2nd bowl, combine: cloves, flour, nutmeg, cinnamon, baking powder, salt, and baking soda.
- Combine both bowls and stir everything then divide the mix between the bread pans.
- Cook the loaves in the oven for about 60 mins or until a toothpick comes out clean when pressed into the middle of each loaf of bread.
- Let the loaves sit on the counter for 15 mins.
- Enjoy.

Amount per serving 12
Timing Information:

Preparation	15 m
Cooking	50 m
Total Time	2 h 35 m

Nutritional Information:

Calories	491 kcal
Fat	26.5 g
Carbohydrates	59.6g
Protein	5.8 g
Cholesterol	46 mg
Sodium	231 mg

* Percent Daily Values are based on a 2,000 calorie diet.

CAJUN CUCUMBERS

Ingredients
- 1/2 C. white vinegar
- 1/2 C. white sugar
- 1/2 tsp Cajun spice
- 1/4 tsp celery seed
- 2 cucumbers, sliced
- 1/4 C. sliced sweet onion

Directions
- Get a bowl, combine: celery seed, vinegar, Cajun spice, and sugar. Combine in the onion and cucumber and place a covering of plastic on the bowl.
- Put everything in the fridge for 7 hours.
- Enjoy.

Amount per serving 4
Timing Information:

Preparation	10m
Cooking	8h
Total Time	8 h 10 m

Nutritional Information:

Calories	116 kcal
Fat	0.2 g
Carbohydrates	29.4g
Protein	0.8 g
Cholesterol	0 mg
Sodium	293 mg

* Percent Daily Values are based on a 2,000 calorie diet.

MONTANA RANCH CUCUMBERS

Ingredients
- 6 C. sliced cucumber
- 1 C. sliced onion
- 1 C. sliced green bell pepper
- 2 tbsps salt
- 1 tbsp celery seed
- 1 C. distilled white vinegar
- 1 1/2 C. white sugar

Directions
- Get a bowl, combine: green peppers, cucumber, and onions.
- Get the following boiling in a pot: sugar, salt, vinegar, and celery seed.
- Once the mix begins to boil, stir it then shut the heat and let the mix sit for 17 mins.
- Mix the cucumber with the vinegar mix then divide everything between jars for storage.
- Place everything in the fridge for an entire day.
- Enjoy.

Amount per serving 32
Timing Information:

Preparation	30 m
Cooking	20 m
Total Time	50 m

Nutritional Information:

Calories	43 kcal
Fat	0.1 g
Carbohydrates	10.8g
Protein	0.3 g
Cholesterol	0 mg
Sodium	437 mg

* Percent Daily Values are based on a 2,000 calorie diet.

WHITE SAUCE OF CUCUMBERS

Ingredients
- 2 small pickling cucumbers, peeled, seeded, and diced
- 1/2 tsp salt
- 2/3 C. low-fat plain yogurt
- 1/2 tsp minced fresh mint leaves
- 1/2 tsp minced fresh dill

Directions
- Get a colander for your cucumber then top the diced cucumber with salt evenly. Let the mix sit for 17 mins.
- Get a bowl, combine: dill, mint, and yogurt. Once the mix is evenly combined add in the cucumber and place a covering of plastic on the bowl put everything in the fridge for 2 hours.
- Enjoy.

Amount per serving 12
Timing Information:

Preparation	15m
Cooking	30m
Total Time	45m

Nutritional Information:

Calories	13 kcal
Fat	0.2 g
Carbohydrates	1.9g
Protein	0.9 g
Cholesterol	< 1 mg
Sodium	107 mg

* Percent Daily Values are based on a 2,000 calorie diet.

CANNING CUCUMBERS

Ingredients
- 2 cucumbers, thinly sliced
- 1/2 C. white vinegar
- 3 tbsps white sugar
- 2 tbsps water
- 1/4 tsp salt
- 2 tbsps minced parsley (optional)

Directions
- Get a bowl for you cucumber.
- Get a 2nd bowl, combine: salt, vinegar, water, and sugar. Stir the mix completely until everything is dissolved then combine the mix with the cucumber/
- Top everything with your parsley. Place the dish in the fridge for 4 hours.
- Enjoy.

Amount per serving 8
Timing Information:

Preparation	10
Cooking	3h
Total Time	3 h 10 m

Nutritional Information:

Calories	29 kcal
Fat	0.1 g
Carbohydrates	7.3g
Protein	0.5 g
Cholesterol	0 mg
Sodium	75 mg

* Percent Daily Values are based on a 2,000 calorie diet.

PUMPERNICKEL PARTY APPETIZER

Ingredients
- 1 (8 oz.) package spreadable cream cheese
- 1/4 C. sour cream
- 1 (.7 oz.) package dry Italian-style salad dressing mix
- 1 (1 pound) loaf sliced pumpernickel party bread
- 2 cucumbers, peeled and thinly sliced
-

Directions
- Get a bowl, combine: dressing mix, sour cream, and cream cheese.
- Coat your pumpernickel with cream cheese evenly then top each piece of bread with some pieces of cucumber.
- Enjoy.

Amount per serving 12
Timing Information:

| Preparation | 10 m |
| Total Time | 10 m |

Nutritional Information:

Calories	186 kcal
Fat	8.7 g
Carbohydrates	21.3g
Protein	5.7 g
Cholesterol	23 mg
Sodium	552 mg

* Percent Daily Values are based on a 2,000 calorie diet.

Stir Fried Kale

Ingredients
- 2 bunches kale, ribs removed and leaves torn into pieces
- 6 tbsps mayonnaise
- 6 tbsps olive oil
- 1/4 C. Dijon mustard
- 1/4 C. grated Parmesan cheese
- lemon, juiced
- 4 tsps minced garlic
- 2 tsps Worcestershire sauce
- 1 tsp anchovy paste
- 1 cucumber, sliced
- 1/4 C. chopped leeks
- freshly cracked black pepper

Directions
- Begin to stir fry your kale in a frying pan with a medium level of heat for 3 mins. Place the kale in a bowl. And put everything in the fridge for 60 mins.
- Get a bowl, combine: anchovy paste, mayo, Worcestershire, olive oil, garlic, mustard, lemon juice, and parmesan.
- Get a 2nd bowl, combine: leeks, cucumber, and kale. Combine both bowls and toss everything evenly then season the dish some black pepper.

- Enjoy.

Amount per serving 4
Timing Information:

Preparation	15 m
Cooking	1h
Total Time	1 h 15 m

Nutritional Information:

Calories	500 kcal
Fat	39.8 g
Carbohydrates	31.7g
Protein	10.5 g
Cholesterol	13 mg
Sodium	853 mg

* Percent Daily Values are based on a 2,000 calorie diet.

CUCUMBER WITH SEOUL (KOREAN KIMCHEE)

Ingredients
- 1 English cucumber, sliced into 3 inch pieces, then each piece cut into 4 more pieces
- 1 tsp kosher salt
- 2 scallions, white and light green parts only, finely chopped
- 2 tbsps rice vinegar
- 2 cloves garlic, finely chopped
- 1/4 inch piece fresh ginger, finely chopped
- 1 tbsp hot chili oil
- 1 tbsp Korean chili powder
- 1 tsp white sugar
- 1/2 tsp fish sauce

Directions
- Get a bowl for your cumber pieces and coat them with the salt evenly. Stir the mix so everything coated nicely then let the cucumber sit for 45 mins. Now remove any excess liquids.
- Get a 2nd bowl, combine: fish sauce, scallions, sugar, vinegar, garlic, chili powder, ginger, and chili oil. Stir the mix evenly.

Easy Cucumber Cookbook

- Combine both bowls then cover the cucumber mix with some plastic wrap. Let the mix sit in the fridge for 1 hour.
- Enjoy.

Amount per serving 6
Timing Information:

Preparation	10 m
Cooking	1h
Total Time	1 h 10 m

Nutritional Information:

Calories	33 kcal
Fat	2.1 g
Carbohydrates	3.9g
Protein	0.6 g
Cholesterol	0 mg
Sodium	366 mg

* Percent Daily Values are based on a 2,000 calorie diet.

New England Tilapia with Tarragon

Ingredients
- 1 tsp salt
- 2 cucumbers, peeled, halved lengthwise, seeded, and chopped
- 1 C. whipping cream
- 2 tbsps prepared mustard
- 2 tsps chopped fresh tarragon
- 2 C. white wine
- salt to taste
- 1 bay leaf
- 2 (3 oz.) fresh tilapia fillets

Directions
- Place your cucumber in a bowl and top them with salt. Let everything stand for 60 mins the remove the liquid.
- Add the following to a pot: tarragon, mustard, and whipping cream. Stir the mix and heat it with a medium level of heat, then add in the cucumber and let everything cook for 10 mins.
- Get a frying pan and add in your wine, bay leaf, and salt. Get everything boiling. Once the mix is boiling place your tilapia

in the frying pan and set the heat to low. Let the fish cook for 9 mins the top the tilapia with the tarragon cucumber mix.

- Enjoy.

Amount per serving 2
Timing Information:

Preparation	10 m
Cooking	10 m
Total Time	1 h 20 m

Nutritional Information:

Calories	754 kcal
Fat	46.1 g
Carbohydrates	21g
Protein	22.6 g
Cholesterol	194 mg
Sodium	1649 mg

* Percent Daily Values are based on a 2,000 calorie diet.

MICHELLE'S CUCUMBER VELVET

Ingredients
- 1 C. heavy cream
- 4 tbsps distilled white vinegar
- salt and pepper to taste
- 1 pinch dried dill, or to taste
- 2 large cucumbers, sliced

Directions
- Get a bowl, combine: dill, cream, pepper, vinegar, and salt. Stir the mix completely then place a covering of plastic on the bowl and put the mix in the fridge for 1 hour.
- Add your sliced cucumber to the sour cream mix and stir everything completely.
- Enjoy.

Amount per serving 4
Timing Information:

Preparation	10 m
Total Time	10 m

Nutritional Information:

Calories	227 kcal
Fat	22.2 g
Carbohydrates	6.9g
Protein	2.2 g
Cholesterol	82 mg
Sodium	26 mg

* Percent Daily Values are based on a 2,000 calorie diet.

Cucumber Freezies

Ingredients
- 2 large cucumbers, thinly sliced
- 2 tbsps salt
- 1 1/2 C. white sugar
- 1 1/2 C. distilled white vinegar

Directions
- Get a bowl for your cucumber. Top them with salt. Place a covering of plastic on the bowl and place everything in the fridge for an entire day.
- Now rinse off the cucumbers and combine with the vinegar and sugar. Place everything in the fridge for another day covered.
- Now place the mix into freezer containers and put everything in the freezer over night until it is all completely frozen.
- Enjoy.

Amount per serving 8
Timing Information:

Preparation	10m
Cooking	2d
Total Time	2 d 10 m

Nutritional Information:

Calories	157 kcal
Fat	0.1 g
Carbohydrates	40g
Protein	0.5 g
Cholesterol	0 mg
Sodium	1746 mg

* Percent Daily Values are based on a 2,000 calorie diet.

ASIAN-FUSION CUCUMBERS

Ingredients
- 1/8 C. red wine vinegar
- 1/4 C. mirin (Japanese sweet wine)
- 1/8 C. packed brown sugar
- 3 tsps grated fresh ginger
- 1/8 C. fresh lime juice
- 1 large cucumber, thinly sliced
- 1/4 C. thinly sliced onion

Directions
- Get a bowl, combine: lime juice, wine vinegar, ginger, brown sugar, and mirin. Stir the mix until it is combined completely then combine in the onion.
- Combine in the onion and cucumber and stir everything completely. Place a covering of plastic on the bowl and put everything in the fridge for 1 hour.
- Enjoy.

Amount per serving 4
Timing Information:

Preparation	45 m
Total Time	45 m

Nutritional Information:

Calories	80 kcal
Fat	0.1 g
Carbohydrates	16.4g
Protein	0.7 g
Cholesterol	0 mg
Sodium	4 mg

* Percent Daily Values are based on a 2,000 calorie diet.

COUNTRY CABIN CUCUMBERS SIDE DISH

Ingredients
- olive oil cooking spray
- 2 tbsps butter, cut into small chunks (optional)
- 1 large cucumber - peeled, seeded, and cut lengthwise into spears
- 1 small sweet onion (such as Vidalia(R)), cut in half and sliced
- 1 tsp chopped fresh basil
- 1 tsp chopped fresh parsley
- 1 tsp chopped fresh cilantro
- 1 tsp chopped fresh mint

Directions
- Cover a casserole dish with foil. Then coat the foil with cooking spray. Set your oven to 350 degrees before doing anything else.
- Dot your casserole dish with pieces of butter then top the pieces of butter with the cucumber and the onion.
- Not top everything with your mint, basil, cilantro, and parsley. Coat everything with some more cooking spray then cook it all in the oven for 12 mins. Flip everything

and continue to cook the dish in the oven for 17 more mins.

- Enjoy.

Amount per serving 4
Timing Information:

Preparation	15 m
Cooking	25 m
Total Time	40 m

Nutritional Information:

Calories	67 kcal
Fat	6 g
Carbohydrates	3.4g
Protein	0.7 g
Cholesterol	15 mg
Sodium	43 mg

* Percent Daily Values are based on a 2,000 calorie diet.

ANDY'S KOREAN STYLE CUCUMBERS WITH HOT SAUCE

Ingredients
- 1 tsp vegetable oil
- 2 tbsps sesame seeds
- 2 tbsps kochujang (Korean hot sauce)
- 1/4 C. white vinegar
- 1 tbsp sesame oil
- 1 green onion, chopped
- 1 cucumber, halved, seeded and thinly sliced

Directions
- Begin to fry your sesame seeds in hot veggie oil for 4 mins. Shut the heat and put everything into a bowl.
- Add the following to the bowl, green onion, Korean hot sauce, sesame oil, and vinegar. Combine everything evenly then combine in the cucumber and stir everything again.
- Enjoy.

Amount per serving 4
Timing Information:

Preparation	10 m
Cooking	5 m
Total Time	15 m

Nutritional Information:

Calories	79 kcal
Fat	6.8 g
Carbohydrates	3.9g
Protein	1.2 g
Cholesterol	0 mg
Sodium	320 mg

* Percent Daily Values are based on a 2,000 calorie diet.

JAPANESE INSPIRED SESAME CUCUMBERS

Ingredients
- 3 large cucumbers - sliced lengthwise, seeds scooped out, and cut into 1/2-inch thick half rounds
- 2 tsps salt
- 1 tbsp soy sauce
- 1 tbsp white sugar
- 3 cloves garlic, thinly sliced
- 2 tsps rice vinegar
- 1 1/2 tsps toasted sesame oil
- 1 tsp hot chili oil
- 1/2 tsp red pepper flakes

Directions
- Get a colander for your cucumber. Top the cucumber with salt and let it sit for 45 mins. Remove an extra juices but do not run it under water.
- Get a bowl, combine: red pepper flakes, soy sauce, chili oil, sugar, sesame oil, garlic, and rice vinegar. Stir the mix then add in your cucumbers and toss everything.
- Place a covering of plastic on the bowl and put everything in the fridge for 4 hrs.
- Enjoy.

Amount per serving 4
Timing Information:

Preparation	15m
Cooking	2h
Total Time	2h15m

Nutritional Information:

Calories	75 kcal
Fat	3.1 g
Carbohydrates	12g
Protein	1.8 g
Cholesterol	0 mg
Sodium	1393 mg

* Percent Daily Values are based on a 2,000 calorie diet.

CUCUMBER TURKEY BITES

Ingredients
- 16 1/2-inch thick slices of cucumber
- 1/2 C. coarsely chopped cooked honey turkey
- 3 tbsps reduced-fat mayonnaise
- 2 tsps Dijon mustard
- 1/2 tsp curry powder

Directions
- Lay out your cucumber slices and with a melon baller take out the middle of the slice to make a cup.
- Get your blender and add in the following: curry powder, turkey, Dijon, and mayo. Process the mix until it is nicely combined and chopped evenly then add about 2 tsps of mix to each piece of cucumber.
- Enjoy.

Amount per serving 16
Timing Information:

Preparation	15 m
Total Time	15 m

Nutritional Information:

Calories	23 kcal
Fat	1.7 g
Carbohydrates	1.1g
Protein	0.9 g
Cholesterol	3 mg
Sodium	89 mg

* Percent Daily Values are based on a 2,000 calorie diet.

WINTER HARVEST SOUP

Ingredients
- 1/2 (12 oz.) package chicken link sausage, casings removed, optional
- 1 (15 oz.) can sweet peas
- 3 C. water
- 2 cucumbers - peeled, seeded, and chopped
- 1 (12 oz.) can evaporated milk
- 2 vegetarian patties, crumbled
- 1/2 C. chopped green bell pepper
- 2 green onions, chopped
- 3 cloves garlic, minced
- 2 cubes chicken bouillon
- 1 tbsp dried dill
- 1 tsp Italian seasoning
- 1 tsp dried parsley
- 1 tsp curry powder
- 1/4 tsp dried thyme
- 1/4 tsp cayenne pepper
- 1/8 tsp celery salt
- 1 bay leaf
- 1/4 C. grated Parmesan cheese, or as needed (optional)

Directions

- Cut your sausages in half lengthwise, then in half again to make 4 long strips and place them into the crock of a slow cooker.
- Puree your peas in a blender until they are smooth then add them with the sausages as well.
- Add in your: bay leaf, water, celery salt, evaporated milk, cayenne, vegetarian patties, thyme, bell pepper, curry powder, green onions, parsley, cucumbers, garlic, Italian spice, dill, and bouillon.
- Stir the mix then it all cook on high for 2.5 hours. Or you can cook this soup in a large pot with a low level of heat for 2.5 hrs as well.
- Top the soup with your parmesan cheese.
- Enjoy.

Amount per serving 10
Timing Information:

Preparation	20 m
Cooking	2 h
Total Time	2 h 20 m

Nutritional Information:

Calories	147 kcal
Fat	8 g
Carbohydrates	10.7g
Protein	9.1 g
Cholesterol	24 mg
Sodium	552 mg

* Percent Daily Values are based on a 2,000 calorie diet.

SUMMER SALAD OF MINT

Ingredients
- 1/3 C. red wine vinegar
- 1 tbsp white sugar
- 1 tsp salt
- 2 large cucumbers, peeled, seeded, and cut into 1/2-inch slices
- 3 large tomatoes, seeded and chopped
- 2/3 C. chopped red onion
- 1/2 C. chopped fresh mint
- 2 tbsps olive oil
- salt and pepper to taste

Directions
- Get a bowl, combine: salt, sugar, and vinegar. Stir the mix until everything has dissolved nicely then combine in the cucumber and stir everything again. Let the mix stand for 60 mins and stir it every 25 mins.
- Add in the olive oil, tomatoes, mint, and onion and stir everything again then add you preferred amount of pepper and salt.
- Enjoy.

Amount per serving 6
Timing Information:

Preparation	15 m
Cooking	1 h
Total Time	1 h 15 m

Nutritional Information:

Calories	88 kcal
Fat	4.8 g
Carbohydrates	11.4g
Protein	1.6 g
Cholesterol	0 mg
Sodium	459 mg

* Percent Daily Values are based on a 2,000 calorie diet.

CUCUMBER FIESTA

Ingredients
- 1/4 C. cider vinegar
- 1 tsp white sugar
- 1/2 tsp salt
- 1/2 tsp chopped fresh dill weed
- 1/4 tsp ground black pepper
- 2 tbsps vegetable oil
- 2 cucumbers, sliced
- 1 C. sliced red onion
- 2 ripe tomatoes, cut into wedges

Directions
- Get a bowl, combine: oil, vinegar, pepper, sugar, dill, and salt. Stir the mix until the sugar has dissolved then add in the tomatoes, onion, and cucumber.
- Stir the salad together then place a covering of plastic on the bowl and let the salad sit for 20 mins.
- Enjoy.

Amount per serving 6
Timing Information:

Preparation	15m
Cooking	15m
Total Time	30m

Nutritional Information:

Calories	71 kcal
Fat	4.7 g
Carbohydrates	6.7g
Protein	1 g
Cholesterol	0 mg
Sodium	199 mg

* Percent Daily Values are based on a 2,000 calorie diet.

July Balsamic Tomatoes Appetizer

Ingredients
- 1 large cucumber, peeled and sliced
- 2 ripe fresh tomatoes, chopped
- 2 tbsps balsamic vinegar
- 2 tbsps olive oil
- salt and pepper to taste

Directions
- Get a bowl and add in your tomatoes and cucumber. Top everything with your balsamic and olive oil. Stir the mix then top it all with some pepper and salt.
- Place everything in the fridge until it cold.
- Then serve.
- Enjoy.

Amount per serving 4
Timing Information:

Preparation	15 m
Total Time	15 m

Nutritional Information:

Calories	84 kcal
Fat	7 g
Carbohydrates	5.3g
Protein	1 g
Cholesterol	0 mg
Sodium	103 mg

* Percent Daily Values are based on a 2,000 calorie diet.

CALIFORNIA LUNCH BOX CUCUMBER TREATS

Ingredients
- 1 ripe avocado, peeled and pitted
- 1/2 C. fresh basil leaves
- 1 tbsp lime juice
- 1 clove garlic
- 1/4 tsp salt
- 1/4 tsp ground black pepper
- 1 cucumber, cut into 1/4-inch slices
- 1 plum tomato, cut into 1/4-inch slices
- 1 tbsp plain yogurt, or to taste (optional)

Directions
- Add the following to a blender and puree it: pepper, avocado, salt, basil, garlic, and lime juice. Puree the mix completely then coat each piece of cucumber with the mix some yogurt and a piece of tomato.
- Enjoy

Amount per serving 4
Timing Information:

| Preparation | 10 m |
| Total Time | 10 m |

Nutritional Information:

Calories	97 kcal
Fat	7.6 g
Carbohydrates	7.8g
Protein	1.9 g
Cholesterol	< 1 mg
Sodium	154 mg

* Percent Daily Values are based on a 2,000 calorie diet.

CANNING CUCUMBERS IN HONG KONG

Ingredients
- 1/2 tsp salt
- 1 large English cucumber, cut into 1/4 inch slices
- 3 tbsps rice vinegar
- 3 tbsps honey

Directions
- Get a colander for your cucumber.
- Top them with salt and stir to evenly coat all the pieces.
- Let the cucumber sit for 40 mins. Drain out he liquid then place everything into a bowl. Combine in your honey and rice vinegar.
- Toss the mix evenly. Place a covering of plastic on the bowl and put everything into the fridge for 60 mins.
- Enjoy.

Amount per serving 4
Timing Information:

Preparation	10m
Cooking	9h30m
Total Time	9 h 40 m

Nutritional Information:

Calories	58 kcal
Fat	0.1 g
Carbohydrates	15.5g
Protein	0.5 g
Cholesterol	0 mg
Sodium	293 mg

* Percent Daily Values are based on a 2,000 calorie diet.

SIMPLY SUSHI

Ingredients
- 1 1/4 C. water
- 1 C. uncooked glutinous white rice (sushi rice)
- 3 tbsps rice vinegar
- 1 pinch salt
- 4 sheets nori (dry seaweed)
- 1/2 cucumber, sliced into thin strips
- 1 avocado - peeled, pitted and sliced

Directions
- Get your rice boiling in water. Place a lid on the pot, set the heat to low, and let the rice cook for 22 mins. Shut the heat and combine in a small amount of salt and the vinegar. Let the rice lose all its heat.
- Lay out a sushi mat and cover it with plastic. Lay out a sheet of seaweed on the mat then lay out some rice evenly on the seaweed sheet. Make sure to not cover an inch of the edge of the seaweed. Place your cucumber strip and avocado in the middle of the rice.
- Roll the seaweed carefully to make a log.
- Continue making sushi logs in this manner until all the ingredients have been used up. With a very sharp knife. Carefully slice it long into 6 - 8 pieces.
- Enjoy.

Amount per serving 6
Timing Information:

Preparation	35 m
Cooking	25 m
Total Time	1 h

Nutritional Information:

Calories	171 kcal
Fat	5.1 g
Carbohydrates	28.7g
Protein	3 g
Cholesterol	0 mg
Sodium	6 mg

* Percent Daily Values are based on a 2,000 calorie diet.

ASIAN CUCUMBER WITH NOODLE

Ingredients
- 1/2 C. white sugar
- 1/4 C. water
- 1 tbsp soy sauce
- 1 tsp ground ginger
- 1 clove garlic, crushed
- 1/2 tsp salt
- 1/2 C. rice vinegar
- 8 oz. Udon noodles, or more to taste
- 2 English cucumbers, sliced
- 1 large shallot, thinly sliced
- 1/2 red bell pepper, thinly sliced
- 1/2 small Thai chili pepper, minced

Directions
- Get the following boiling in a small pot: salt, sugar, garlic, water, ginger, and soy sauce. Let the mix boil for 7 mins while stirring.
- Shut the heat and let it sit for 10 mins.
- Combine in your rice vinegar and stir. This is will be your dressing.
- Get a 2nd large pot filled with water boiling. Once the water is boiling add in your Udon and stir the noodles. Let everything cook for 11 mins then remove the liquid. Run

the noodles under some cold water then place them in a bowl.

- Combine the cucumber with the noodles then also add in: chili pepper, bell pepper, and shallot. Toss everything evenly then combine the dressing with the noodles and toss everything.
- Let the noodles sit for 30 mins.
- Enjoy.

Amount per serving 4
Timing Information:

Preparation	20 m
Cooking	15 m
Total Time	1 h

Nutritional Information:

Calories	296 kcal
Fat	1 g
Carbohydrates	66.6g
Protein	5.7 g
Cholesterol	0 mg
Sodium	858 mg

* Percent Daily Values are based on a 2,000 calorie diet.

3-Brother's Antipasto

Ingredients
- 2 cucumbers - peeled, seeded, and cubed
- 10 cherry tomatoes, quartered
- 10 pitted kalamata olives
- 1/2 pound deli chicken breast, diced into strips
- 1/2 pound fresh mozzarella cheese, cubed
- 1/2 C. Italian-style salad dressing

Directions
- Get a bowl, combine: mozzarella, cucumber, chicken, tomatoes, and olives. Top everything with your dressing and stir the salad to coat everything evenly.
- Place the mix in the fridge to chill.
- Enjoy.

Amount per serving 8
Timing Information:

| Preparation | 15 m |
| Total Time | 15 m |

Nutritional Information:

Calories	194 kcal
Fat	14.1 g
Carbohydrates	5.9g
Protein	10.4 g
Cholesterol	38 mg
Sodium	733 mg

* Percent Daily Values are based on a 2,000 calorie diet.

CUCUMBER CAYENNE MAYO

Ingredients
- 1 (8 oz.) package cream cheese, softened
- 1 cucumber - peeled, seeded, and chopped
- 2 green onions (white part only), chopped
- 1 tbsp milk
- 1 tbsp mayonnaise
- 1/2 tsp cayenne pepper
- 1/4 tsp lemon pepper

Directions
- Get a bowl, combine: lemon pepper, cream cheese, cayenne, cucumber, mayo, milk, and green onions. Stir the mix until it smooth. Place everything in an airtight container for storage in the fridge.
- Enjoy.

Amount per serving 16
Timing Information:

Preparation	15 m
Total Time	15 m

Nutritional Information:

Calories	58 kcal
Fat	5.6 g
Carbohydrates	0.9g
Protein	1.2 g
Cholesterol	16 mg
Sodium	55 mg

* Percent Daily Values are based on a 2,000 calorie diet.

CREAM CHEESE CUCUMBER SAUCE

Ingredients
- 4 oz. cream cheese, softened
- 4 oz. sour cream
- 1/2 large cucumber, peeled and diced
- 1 clove garlic, minced
- 1/4 small onion, diced
- salt and pepper to taste

Directions
- Get a bowl, combine: sour cream and cream cheese. Stir the mix completely then combine in the pepper, cucumber, salt, onion, and garlic. Stir the mix again then place a covering of plastic on the bowl and put everything in the fridge until it is cold.
- Enjoy.

Amount per serving 16
Timing Information:

Preparation	15 m
Total Time	15 m

Nutritional Information:

Calories	42 kcal
Fat	4 g
Carbohydrates	0.9g
Protein	0.8 g
Cholesterol	11 mg
Sodium	25 mg

* Percent Daily Values are based on a 2,000 calorie diet.

LUNCH BOX RANCH SANDWICHES

Ingredients
- 1 C. mayonnaise
- 1 (.7 oz.) package dry Ranch-style salad dressing mix
- 1 (1 pound) loaf cocktail rye bread
- 1 cucumber, peeled and thinly sliced

Directions
- Get a bowl, combine: ranch dressing mix, and mayo.
- Lay out your pieces of rye bread then place a tsp dollop of the mix onto each piece of bread.
- Spread the mix evenly over the entire piece of rye then top each piece of bread with a piece of cucumber.
- Enjoy.

Amount per serving 15

Timing Information:

Preparation	20 m
Total Time	20 m

Nutritional Information:

Calories	110 kcal
Fat	11.7 g
Carbohydrates	1.5g
Protein	0.2 g
Cholesterol	6 mg
Sodium	296 mg

* Percent Daily Values are based on a 2,000 calorie diet.

Thanks for Reading! Join the Club and Keep on Cooking with 6 More Cookbooks....

http://bit.ly/1TdrStv

 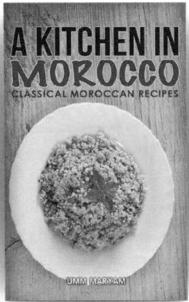 

To grab the box sets simply follow the link mentioned above, or tap one of book covers.

This will take you to a page where you can simply enter your email address and a PDF version of the box sets will be emailed to you.

Hope you are ready for some serious cooking!

http://bit.ly/1TdrStv

COME ON...
LET'S BE FRIENDS :)

We adore our readers and love connecting with them socially.

Like BookSumo on Facebook and let's get social!

Facebook

And also check out the BookSumo Cooking Blog.

Food Lover Blog

Printed in Great Britain
by Amazon